Learning to Share

Kids Book

Share by Asking and Giving

With Powerful Activities for Kids and Toddlers.

By

Steve Glenn

SHARE

My name is Rex and I love to share my story. It's time to share.

what does sharing really mean?

What is sharing?

Does it mean to keep all your things to yourself without giving?

Like having lots of crayons but refusing to share?

Sharing means to give. it also means to exchange.

Salma was walking down the ever-
busy road as It was a rainy day. She
saw a helpless dog and decided to
help out.

Why do We share?

When we share our things with our friends and brothers, it shows that we care.

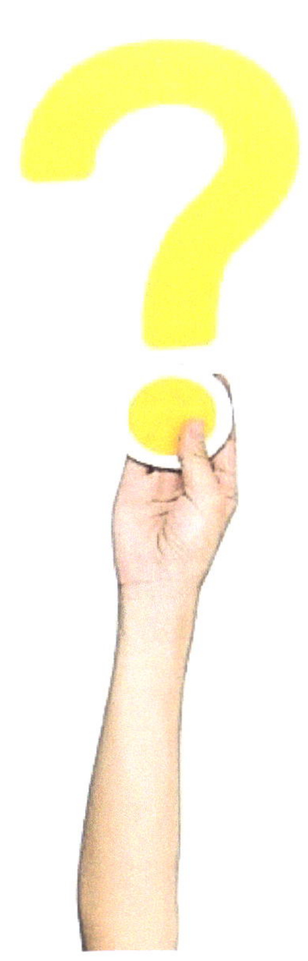

For example, sharing your candy

Sharing helps you make friends easily.

When you share with others, you become friends with them. And it gives us that deep happy feelings.

So, Let's Practice How to SHARE

Practice?
Practise?

You can read together and have fun

doing so.

Let's play football,

You can share food and other things
with your brothers and siblings.

Share our dance steps. this makes us

a better two.

Sharing   makes   us   all   happy

You can share your story book with a friend

SHARING ACTIVITIES

ACTIVITY ONE

The Shiny Apple activity

Number of persons we need: 2 - 8 kids

Things You Need: An apple (either real or fake)

Instructions

1. Ask the kids to sit in a circle.

2. Choose someone that will hold the apple first. Then share by passing it.

3. Start singing "Shiny apple, shiny apple, who's got the shiny apple? If you've got the shiny apple, you have won!"

4. Anyone holding the apple when the song ends is the winner. He will hold the apple first as the next round begins.

5. Do this several times.

ACTIVITY TWO

Chopped-Preschool Version

Number of Participants: 3 to 5 kids and some grown-ups

What You Need: Kitchen supplies, mystery ingredients, and of course, a kitchen

Instructions

1. Tell some friends and bring them to your kitchen for this competition. When you send invitations, include a list of secret ingredients.

2. Let them come with 1 or 2 secret ingredients. These should be enough; so ensure that every family comes with more quantity. As friends come around, place the ingredients into a closed basket.

3. When they have all arrived, gather around a large place or table so every child has a set of utensils and dishes.
4. Ready and Shout 'Go' so each child should create a dish using just the ingredients in the basket. Some Kids will have to share ingredients.
5. After 12 minutes, take turns tasting what they have made.

How does this teach them about Sharing?

This fun activity assists them in developing their kitchen skills, their eating habits and sharing culture. Since they have to share the ingredients available which each family has brought. In addition, this will assist them in valuing in a group work as they taste the dishes they made.

ACTIVITY THREE

Mix And Match The Eggs

We Shall Use All Our Easter Plastic Eggs As They Will Be Suitable For This Exercise

Therefore, in this activity, kids need to share half of their egg to make a whole egg of the same color.

Number of Participants: 2 - 10

What You Need: Assorted plastic eggs

Instructions

1. Rearrange the eggs before you begin so you have two different colors. For this age group, the activity will work best if you exchange halves on two eggs of different colors. For instance, paint one egg with a blue top and purple bottom and another with purple top and blue bottom.

2. Divide the eggs evenly among the participants.

3. Let them sit in a circle.

4. Read out the Instructions. By saying that the we shall be playing this game to make each of your eggs become a single color.

5. Let them begin by asking each other for the color he needs for a particular egg. For example, if you have an egg with a green top and a red bottom, ask the person with a green and red egg to exchange bottoms with you.

6. Keep going round the circle until each person has completed his task.

What we learn from this activity

It teaches kids to ask for help from others before they can finish the task. This is one gain of sharing as they help each other reach a goal.

ACTIVITY FOUR

The Shared Treasure Hunt

Treasure hunts are a fun way for your kids to go on adventure.

And this can be adapted to any age group. This allows kids the opportunity to help and share different things with their friends. When it's completed, everyone gets a prize. You will have to plan and prepare.

Number of Participants: 2 - 4 kids

What You Need: Pre-made clues, a large shareable prize

Instructions

1. Get the index cards or scraps of paper, add some pictures of various items or locations within your house. Choose big and obvious pictures of varied items any child should be conversant with in sort of a

couch or bed. When possible, use an image that the majorly or closely resembles the color of your actual items because kids during this age bracket tend to think literally.

2. Make a group of cards for every child, using an equivalent item in each set. Rearrange the order of things in each set, but have all of them end within the same place. For instance, one child may need to seek out the couch, then the toilet and end at the table while another starts at the toilet, then goes to the couch and ends at the table.

3. Set by set, hide the clues within the appropriate locations.

4. Once each child has found all of his clues, he should meet the opposite kids at the designated end spot.

5. **If kids grind to a halt, they will ask one another for help.**

6. Once all of them reach the top place, they will share the prize.

ACTIVITY FIVE

Let's Go Fishing

This activity helps kids to find a partner to finish the charade of fisherman and fish.

Number of Participants: 6 to 20.

What You Need: A large place for kids to run.

Instructions

1. Ask all kids to run in a circle going the same direction.

2. When you shout "Go Fishing," kids will try to find a partner and take the correct stance, and someone standing with arms extended in front like a fishing pole, the other person laying on the ground in front flapping like a fish.

3. Everyone who makes it wins the game.

4. Do this several times. Encourage kids to look for a different partner each round.

www.ingramcontent.com/pod-product-compliance
Lightning Source LLC
Chambersburg PA
CBHW040318240726
48664CB00006B/1531